How to Resolve Your Resolve

A Reflection on Resilience, Change, and Becoming

Jacques L. Gourdet

Paperback ISBN: 979-8-9951752-0-9

Hardback ISBN: 979-8-9951752-1-6

E-Book ISBN: 979-8-9951752-2-3

To God, my beloved family, and my dear friends - Thank you for inspiring me, standing by me, and believing in me.

Table of Contents

Introduction

I used to live my life in a way that made me proud, accomplished, and respected, until I didn't. I felt like I had no limits and all the potential in the world to achieve my dreams, until I didn't. I felt unstoppable and could overcome anything, until I was stopped and felt I could do nothing. Life threw a setback my way that I couldn't see coming, and it destroyed my confidence, pride, and ambition. I became paralyzed, disabled, and bedridden due to an extremely rare infection brought on by an extremely common flu.

Although it might seem that luck was not on my side, given that this type of event occurs in only 3 out of every 100,000 patient-years (a 0.003% incidence rate), I disagree. A neuro-immunological disorder called Transverse Myelitis, so rare that many doctors will never encounter it in their careers, took from me. I rate my pain as a 7 out of 10 on my best days. I struggle to remember things without a lot of effort and tools, let alone learn, which was once my favorite activity. My immune system is like having a plastic bag for a windshield. My professional life ended, triggering an identity crisis. All my prospects vanished in moments, leaving long-term effects. I lost many things that defined me, and in turn, lost myself.

Despite all of this, where there was sadness, I have joy; where there was conflict, I have peace; and where there was fear, I have hope and the courage to hope. I am one of the faceless people I used to think about. I mean those who live a life I could not imagine due to the difficulty, lack of resources, or inability to escape it. I did not know how the faceless could smile despite facing such adversity. I did not understand how so many people in our world could face such challenges and still find happiness.

Therefore, I have written these short lessons to help in the pursuit of a hopefully long, satisfying, and happy life.

I believe that, having learned as I have, it makes sense to share the easier way to come to terms with oneself. I believe that happiness is not found but realized. I believe we tend to get so busy that we become woefully unaware of what is right in front of our eyes. I also believe that everyone can come to a true understanding of who they are and who they want to be. Processing the right questions and the sometimes unavoidably painful but honest answers is key.

I have included my own thoughts and experiences to reflect on and hopefully inspire you to ponder your own. My experiences and thoughts will serve as a guide as I encountered discomfort, defeat, and discovery. Read through, ask yourself questions, commit to answering them honestly, adjust as needed, and start over. This will begin a process or pattern of thinking that leads to a cycle of change. Much like when a piece of metal is being forged, the process often involves intense heat, dedicated coaxing, and a transformation beyond what the eyes can fully see, much less grasp. There will be soul-searching and soul-answering. You will be asked questions that may be rhetorical, figurative, and/or literal. As with myself, asking questions to gauge knowledge can only get oneself so far. However, asking questions about one's experience goes much further. As such, when you come to an actionable realization, strike while the iron is hot. Our situations may be vastly different, but deep down, our internal conflicts, motivations, and concerns are often the same.

I have realized joy, peace, courage, hope, and more despite the difficulty of the way I came. I do not think it is necessary to suffer to learn, grow, and live a fulfilling life. I think there is an easier way. It only requires an open mind, truth in vulnerability, and the willingness to examine another's experience as your own. I want to ease the way for others, so they do not have to go through what I have been through to find their way, if only sooner.

If you are feeling weak, lost, alone, and/or scared, then I am writing for you. I know that all these feelings and more can bring dread if we let them. It is a pleasure to show you how to steel yourself, empower yourself, ground yourself, and find the resolve to live your best despite the worst.

Chapter 1:

Obsidian Shards

Experience:

I did not know anyone going through bankruptcy, much less ever thought I would experience it myself. I had no idea what it would feel like to be stripped of my dignity and discover the stinging pain of stigma and shame that comes when you are judged as financially incapable. I did not think that I would ever arrive here, being seized upon by the jaws of financial disorder.

I could not fathom that I would ever be in a position where I felt helpless as to the resources that I had. I was raised to make my own way, make my own decisions, and be accountable. I always thought that if I did everything with honesty and integrity, I would be protected from dangers I believed followed only those who made the wrong decisions.

I was without income because I could not work, despite how hard I tried. I sat with my briefcase next to my recliner, my computer propped up, my phone in hand, and my Bluetooth headset firmly affixed to my ear, and nothing came. I sat there for many hours desperately trying to think of anything and everything I could to stop the spiral of destruction happening around me.

I couldn't help but think about my recent past, when I worked hard for my acclaim, reputation, and financial stability. These thoughts crossed my mind between the urges I desperately fought not to scream from the unyielding pain I was feeling. I frantically tried to figure out what was wrong with me between visits to neurologists, neuro-musculoskeletal specialists, and many other doctors. The jumble of medical jargon I heard from visit to visit was, at best, hard to understand and, at worst, completely repulsive. The only words I wanted to hear were, "We have a solution for you, and you will be feeling better shortly."

My not being able to move my legs, escape the physical pain that was robbing me of the will to live, and the strange fog in my head preventing me from being able to think was too much. There was far too much chaos happening, I thought, but like everything else, I figured that would be the worst of it, and then things would go back to normal. It never occurred to me that some problems do not present with an end but present as a beginning.

My new normal consisted of me being prescribed many muscle relaxants daily, searching the internet for answers my doctors could not give me, and trying to figure out what I could do in my current state to keep my home. The fear that gripped me made my eyes twitch, my mouth run dry, and my heart feel like it was standing still. The idea of being out on the street in a box became a reality in my head, not just something I kept locked away as an irrational fear.

I worked hard and became strong enough to prevent the terrible reality I envisioned: no home, no car, no income, and no way out. I knew that I could always count on myself to keep the words overdue, late, final notice, rejected, collections, urgent, and failure away. I knew that if I fought for my stability, the wolves of collection would never come scratching at my door.

When my health was taken out of the equation and my days weren't spent working on a project or proposal, but simply on getting to the next day, certain things became clear. I knew I was in trouble. I also knew I couldn't get through this on my own, no matter how hard I tried. I came to the humbling realization that I might never stand tall on my own two feet again.

In my plight, I called on family and friends for support and financial and emotional stability, as I could no longer provide for myself. They showed up in ways that helped manage the pressure until I was acclimated to it. The paralysis of thought was gone, and I knew that what I had, whatever I had left, needed to be devoted to the struggle.

My pride was shattered, but I felt deeply humbled and grateful to realize there was somehow a way forward. I mostly focused on what I could do for myself instead of everything else, and I found options. I didn't want to consider starting over from scratch. I didn't want to think about losing the assets I had before. I didn't want to imagine losing the freedom to go and do as I please. I didn't want to think of a simpler, reduced, and more refined life.

I did the things I did not want to do out of necessity, to focus on the more important ones: to keep living, keep dreaming, and keep trying. I kept trying, kept going, and kept dreaming! I am alive today because of the struggles I thought I could never overcome. The issues that seemed like a wall have been broken down many times. I know that no matter where I start, I will keep going to reach my beautiful end. Along the way, I have found people I am forever grateful for, stories I would never have heard, and a strength I could never have summoned if I did not keep moving forward.

I am happier than I have ever been, I am stronger, and even though I may not always be physically prepared to face what's in front of me, I am emotionally ready. The entirety of who I am will

follow wherever my mind guides it. I
continue…

Reflection:

Have you ever wondered what your life
would be like if you lost everything?
Who would you become? What would
you do? Does the very thought trigger an
anxiety you bury so deep that it is only
examined for seconds at a time? I never
imagined being paralyzed both
figuratively and literally, not to mention
in multiple areas. I will tell you what
used to define everything for me and
what happened to that anxiety.

For most people, the definition of
everything includes, but is not limited to,
money, control, power, status, and

security. Losing these things feels like losing a part of oneself. This is how I felt when I lost the outer layer of protection I wore to shield me from the world's gaze and judgment. Losing these things is like being left exposed to the world and to all the threats we desperately try to keep away. Along the way, it was instilled in me that, I am what I have, and if I have nothing, I am nothing.

These things I seek are equivalent to life's greatest achievements. Having plenty of them will bring me the highest happiness we can experience. We are told that without these things, we will be trapped in an endless maze of forgotten darkness. Without our version of everything, we will face an ironic living death devoid of happiness and self-fulfillment. This means a life has no meaning without these prized possessions and the proper level of socio-economic status.

Let's reflect on the living afterlife for just a moment. How do the blind see the sunset better than those with sight? How do the deaf hear the chorus of birds in the distance when those who hear cannot? How does one who cannot stand, run, while the world abound has only braced itself to crawl? How can someone have nothing and yet have everything? How can the frail be champions in life's arena? How does one shout without a voice? How does one feel without nerves?

I came to understand that things might not be all they were made out to be. I also realized that things can be replaced and that you do not have to look very far to find anyone else who has them. I further realized that we tend to focus on things that are replaceable, all the while ignoring the things that we can't.

When my life blew up, it sent shockwaves throughout my entire world. Like a volcanic eruption, the molten lava of tragedy hurled itself at everything I cherished, scorching the rest so quickly I couldn't react emotionally in time. Stability, security, a clear path, and certainty — things I relied on — were destroyed and I was on fire. Why did everything I tried to do end up like this? What kind of silver lining can I see when my sky is darkened by falling ash?

From death comes life or a transition to a new beginning. The same lava that incinerated the ground creates new land that never existed before. The same burning ash raining down destruction from above contributes to a flood of life below. The area, once thick with choking smoke and noxious gas, becomes clear, clean, and hospitable. Where all life was made to flee from getting caught in the waves of terraforming punishment, they are invited to return to lush, rich, and promising possibilities.

I ultimately discovered that, beneath all the burdens and responsibilities I heaped upon myself, I was missing things that were truly important to me. I was missing out on talking to my family early and often about myself and about them. I was missing out on opportunities to be a true friend and provide actual support to those friends. I was missing out on being there for a rising generation that, more than ever, needs guidance to navigate the unique challenges they are facing. I was missing out on cultivating myself or putting in the emphasis on self-growth. I was missing out on participating in my own life. I was busy replacing relationships, people, and personal growth with things, temporary rewards, and self-placating experiences to distract or make me feel better for not devoting myself to the former. And so, are life-altering events always an elemental disaster, or can they present as an opportunity?

I suspect that whether our own decisions trigger an event or it happens naturally, there are reasons to pause. Re-evaluating how we spend our time is not the worst idea. Events that tend to stop us in our tracks, as they ruin our plans, provoke us to truly think. When we actually stop to take an inventory of where we are spending our time, energy, and potential, then we can change for the better. Sometimes the old landscape must be done away with for us to embrace the new.

Chapter 2:

Circle the Wagons

Experience:

My life felt like it was over. I sought out emergency treatment because of the flu, and was given some steroids, antibiotics, an over-the-counter pain reliever, and released to go home. 10 days later, I never walked again… I was gripped by pain I had never imagined before. I felt like ants were racing up and down my legs, muscles seizing with electric current, waves of blistering heat and numbing cold washing over, and an unpredictable yet consistent dance of spasms across my lower body. I did not know that I had exchanged the ironic comfort of temporary pain for the relentless company of chronic.

I was a working man, an ordinary man by most accounts, I thought. I had never encountered anything like an autoimmune disorder in my own life, much less have ever heard of such a thing as *Transverse Myelitis*. Something so random and mysterious at the time left me questioning my entire reality. My sanity was driven to the absolute limit as the pain never stopped gnawing, my thoughts could not run away from what was happening to me, and I felt painfully unprepared for the situation that had inflicted a debilitating blow to my life.

My pain kept me company as I watched my life fall apart around me. My mind refused to start, like a car twitching as it tried to wake up through the ignition. The memory I had relied on for everything had failed me. I started losing memories like water circling a drain, then being pulled down into a place with no return. My identity was left in question as I could not work, I could not reliably sleep, and I was trapped in a state of being that could only take and not give, which was unbearable to me.

Without my ability to focus on much besides my mind-altering pain, I felt like I was lost to the world and was nothing. The last thing I ever wanted to be was a burden on anyone around me. I built my life, my personality, and my appearance on being reliable, resourceful, and successful. And yet, despite all my life experiences, in the blink of an eye, I was a stranger to myself and an enemy.

I did not like who I was now, as this was not a provider. This was not the man I said I was. This was not the winner I had proclaimed to be. Watching what was left of my silent bank account seep out, the hard-earned money left me feeling mentally paralyzed in addition to physically. What was I anymore without my identity? What could I do if I could not do for myself? I was known to be able to pivot, figure out a plan in a hurry, and recover from losses or emergencies, but I was not prepared for the emergency to be me.

I could no longer lie down in my own bed anymore, as my legs were locked in spasticity and needed support against gravity. Because of this, the only solution I had at the time was an old brown recliner. It took 5 months to receive my diagnosis, and then longer to receive medical equipment, such as a hospital bed. So, I was confined to a quickly broken recliner as my permanent spot, except during hospital stays, doctor visits, and trips to the bathroom.

I watched the sky turn dark, and present company leave as the world fell asleep. Everything felt eerily silent as I felt detached from everyone and everything. The blue light from a computer was dull, the sound of a TV was pulled into a vacuum, and my reality was being drawn into it all. The only thing I could focus on was the corner of a window to the outside world that I couldn't even reach. It was not completely covered by the curtain, revealing a sliver of the outside, so I could see the color of the sky.

I was haunted by my thoughts of failure, regret, and loneliness. I thought that I would only have to suffer them in the dark of night while everyone else slept, but somehow, they followed me. They did not leave me alone and seemed bent on taking away every happy thought, impression, and memory. And what they could not take, they wanted to twist or corrupt as to convert me from an optimist into a pessimist.

Without the professional armor and weapons of a strong self-image, I was woefully unprepared to engage with the terrors that stayed on me like shadows. Being attacked from all directions by my own self-doubt, self-disgust, and by my disdain for who I was made me so tired. I did not have it in me to defend myself against myself anymore. I started to believe that I was unworthy, no longer a real man, a drain on society, a waste, and devoid of value to anyone.

When I reached my lowest point, I finally reached out because I believed, deep in my memory, that somehow, someway, there were people out there who could love me even if I didn't love myself. I was met with smiles, reminders, hugs—both mental and physical—and the warm embrace of happiness that brought a smile to my face. I was reminded that I knew how to smile before I ever earned my first dollar, received my first reward, graduated from my first program, got my first promotion, or accomplished anything I was proud of. I knew how to laugh before I ever uttered my first word. I knew how to giggle through my tears before I understood what tears meant. The tears that now wet my face are not tears of sadness but of happiness and pride for those who stood with me and for me. I can smile because they knew and loved the version of me that I didn't. I knew that if they could love that version of me, or this one, then I could love myself, too. I knew I could remember their words, hear their voices, and call on them to help me love myself. I knew that with them, I could begin a journey to become a happier version of myself.

Reflection:

Have you ever felt figuratively alone despite literally being surrounded by others during a crisis? How often has the presence of a stranger diminished feelings of danger? Has the logic of the large number of those around you going through the same made you feel better? Know that you and I are not alone in understanding peril that isolates the mind and rattles the heart. Relentless fears, thoughts, and emotions that stalk you during the day and keep you restless during the night. These persistent threats seem to be lying in wait for the worst possible time for you, right? And when you least hoped it would happen, though you have been expecting it, you are taken down with such ferocity that you question your reality altogether.

I wondered in the moments that followed how this could have happened to me. I tried to trace the logic to see where and how it all went wrong. I thought about the rules that the threats were surely following. I thought about the natural laws that surely governed their existence and made their limitations clear. I really thought I had it all figured out, and then I thought that at worst, maybe someone else would be able to come to my aid before a pounce could come my way. I really thought that safety in numbers was the way, and that as a part of the herd, I could avoid being singled out. My false sense of security gave me confidence for threats from the outside, but completely blinded me as to the threats from the inside.

As it turns out, we protect ourselves even from one another by limiting how many people we allow into our hearts. The world is not always a place where everyone treats others as they would like to be treated. This results in very few trusted people having access to our hearts, out of necessity to avoid risk. Yet, even after all the effort to keep the untrustworthy out, we still face the heartbreak of having to revoke access again and again. The optimist in me once believed that life would be filled with the closest of friends. The realist in me has realized that fear, even among those we want to be close to, drives us to walk the path alone. Do we do this because it's better, or because it's easier?

Can we afford not to take the risk of letting anyone in? Have times gotten easier or harder to shoulder burdens? Is the advancement of time always kind to the tired and weary? Are we immune to becoming tired and weary in the first place? Can we really live in this world alone? If you could have significant support present at a specific pivotal time or event in your past, present, or future, which would it be? Are there 3 instances at minimum where that support would make all the difference for you?

Does the need for a relationship with a trusted individual or individuals manifest immediately or gradually? Is it likely that we can predict when such a relationship will become a saving grace? Can we predict how frequently the need for support will test our relationships?

I never could have predicted that I would one day find myself limited to a wheelchair and a hospital bed. I could never have predicted the effect the pain of losing my former life would have on me, nor the pain of living the present. I did not know how lonely I could feel in a situation where many others either avoid me or just do not know what to say. To struggle against a submerging self-worth while dealing with multiple challenging situations took its toll on me. The rules that had made me feel confident in myself had been reset and kept changing as I inched closer to my new normal. Paraplegia, neurological mishaps, and a weakening grasp on time set the stage for my worst nightmares to hunt me during the night and during the day. A fear of failure, all too real, became all-consuming as I felt that I had failed at everything and could never amount to anything. The blows, thrown my way for feeling useless, kept on coming from every direction. I could not determine a defensive position to block the shots or minimize the pain that came with them.

I was taking punches, I was taking kicks, I was hit with objects, and I was humiliated. My emotions, fears, and concerns had assembled into a gang intent on taking me apart. And in the moments when I was being crowded out, my family came to my rescue. I was outnumbered, and they were outnumbered, but together we held our own until the numbers lessened and the threats began to flee. My family, my people, my friends, waited on me until I could rise again and did not leave my side until they were sure I was ok. They reaffirmed to me that if I were ever in danger again, I only needed to summon the courage to call, and they would invoke their love to answer.

I did not always have the luxury of having blood relatives by my side to support me during the harder moments, and that is ok. I came to realize that blood is not family, family is family. If there are no relatives, then we have friends, and friends are the family that we choose. Those with whom we can share our trust and have our best interests at heart are, at their core, the best we can hope to have. While a direct relative may offer deeper understanding of your history, physical makeup, and predispositions, the love that is offered by chosen family can be just as strong, if not stronger.

Would a true loved one prefer that you struggle alone with something that they could help with? Would someone who cares offer their time, effort, or means to help you when you are in need? If the matter of your struggle is not well understood by them, would a true loved one educate themselves about it? Are you the kind of person who would be willing to do the same, and why? Would you slap someone with judgment or extend your hand in compassion when they are struggling? Who can you call that will genuinely answer and rush to your side?

Life is not simple. There are a variety of struggles that can present themselves at almost any given time. The worst kinds always seem to be those we have little to no control over. Those struggles do not appear when it's convenient, easy, or you are feeling prepared. There is little fairness about the fights that can take place, especially where our mental health is concerned. We will be outnumbered, our minds will play tricks on us, and our thoughts will fight dirty. What is it worth to risk falling alone when we can win standing together?

We are strong when we call. Our loved ones are stronger when we answer. We are strongest when we accept.

Chapter 3:

Confined or Liberated

Experience:

I dragged myself to the bathroom for the sake of the little dignity I still had. I couldn't let this be taken from me, too. Day and night, no matter what it took, I would pull myself forward, lunging ahead while holding onto a walker supported by my shoulders and arms.

The life I led in the basement of my home was never something I imagined for myself. I stayed there so long that I had forgotten what the upstairs of my home looked like. The place I had spent all my time in, along with the space I ignored, had completely reversed. I went from seeing people every day and moving among them to being genuinely afraid of them. I was afraid of the reminder of what I had lost and who I had become.

I became afraid that I would be left behind in my current state and have no place left where I was relevant in this world. While I struggled for basic necessities and human dignity in the lowest level of my home, the world kept turning. Others were still achieving great things, while I could not even wash my own clothes.

To wonder whether I would have the strength to make it back 25 feet from where I started was an all-consuming thought. I could not help but laugh at the irony of thinking this way, given that I used to effortlessly move hundreds, and even thousands, of feet. How funny it is that I never thought I could be in a position where the things I once did every day with incredible ease became nearly impossible with my greatest effort.

I thought I was struggling in other ways back then. I really did not realize how much more creative life's struggles could become. Using my arms in place of my legs and having my shoulders take the hits was painful. Wondering if this was the very last time I could do it. Wondering if this was the last time I would have the opportunity.

I was shocked to discover that not only did the struggle not stop, but that it became easier. Day in and day out, I kept pulling myself up and through. What was once an desperate plunge became a swift stride. I became more efficient at preventing injury and keeping myself from registering the pain.

My pain did not diminish during this time, but my awareness increased. I endured transitions that saw me go from completely stationary to partially mobile, and then to fairly mobile. I was able to receive a wheelchair that was appropriately sized to fit through my doorways. The days of burning my toes, chipping, and causing ingrown toenails had finally come to an end. The days of navigating the world in my wheelchair were about to begin.

My fear of the outside slowly faded as I developed a love for nature documentaries and wilderness survival shows. I started to realize that I could see even more of the world than I had before, even when I was fully able-bodied. I could escape into the images of Elephants travelling vast distances with their calves. I could imagine the heights overlooking nature's most lush valleys below. I could peer into the depths of the ocean and see life that many of us working day to day could not. I saw beauty that I did not know existed. I felt the smooth yet rippling waters hugging my fingers. I felt the cool dews that settled on the underbrush before dawn. I saw the shift of the animals change as the day walkers went to sleep and the nocturnal came to life. I heard the birds' call echoing through the trees in countries I may never be fortunate enough to see in person. The vibrance of life sharpened richly when I sought freedom, and I was rewarded with perspective. I was here in my broken recliner, then in my hospital bed, and then in the world. My gaze was stuck, unable to escape the white grooves of my downstairs ceiling, but no longer. My mind was trapped in my body until my body released my mind. I have traveled mentally, voyaged emotionally, and was prepared to keep showing up physically.

I believe that sometimes you must slow down in order to speed up. This became especially relevant as I had to observe every angle to prevent damage to myself, others, and our property. I no longer had the luxury of blindly moving through space with little awareness, nor did I want to after realizing what I had done to this world. One moment of inattention could result in pinched fingers, stubbed toes, deep scratches, bruised calves, broken bones, or worse.

And while having to be so deliberate about my movements was stressful at first, it opened up the possibility of interacting with the world at large again, in a similar but very different way. I could not help but wonder what I had missed before while I was so busy moving that I did not realize the value in being still. I wanted to see at a pace that I had not seen before, carefully, and deliberately taking in the life's wonders around me.

I was able to travel again, like I once did, in a similar but different way. I discovered wheelchair assistance, special checks by airport security, and accommodations both present and missing. Being ushered through the bustling crowds of briskly walking and leisurely strolling passengers brought back a rich sense of normalcy.

My connection to the world had not been broken but, altered. Just as well, my desire to live my life was not lost but found somewhere I did not remember placing it. My idea of freedom was defined by my ability to move freely in space, free from physical limitations. My new idea of freedom was defined by my creativity, my desire to overcome my limitations, and the work needed to make the impossible then possible now. Where I found a secular end, I discovered a spiritual beginning. Where I discovered a physical limit, I discovered an emotional and mental breakthrough. What was the point of walking before, living without all this pain, and having all of my dignity intact if it meant that I could not appreciate what I do now?

Reflection:

Have you ever felt uncomfortable with silence? The quiet anticipation of what's next, the building anxiety, the waning patience, and the thoughts you want to avoid gradually becoming your audience. The crowd begins to grow, more and more arrive, and before long, you are being heckled, jeered at, and threatened on your own stage. The irony is that you can't run because it's a stage of your own making, and it's always a sold-out show. After what can seem like years but only lasts seconds to minutes, someone else enters your focus and frees you from the illusion inside your head.

Having been paralyzed, isolated, and misunderstood, I have felt utterly trapped inside my own mind more times than I could count. I would try to sleep away the silence, play away the silence, tv away the silence. Yet, despite my best efforts, it would trap me in a mental loop of torment, often cycling through my regrets, past mistakes, and failures. So not only was I literally paralyzed, but I also became mentally paralyzed, emotionally paralyzed, and trapped in other ways that I would not wish upon any enemy. I could not run even if I wanted to, and the peace came only when the silence was broken up by very few interactions, often limited to those who paid me a visit.

What would you pay to not have to sit in a cell being rattled by a vindictive warden, a cruel jailer, a mean guard, a taunting punisher? What would you pay to be free from a place where time has no meaning, and all sentences are simply until? What would you do for a taste of freedom that you once called your own? What would you do to see the sky again, breathe fresh air, feel the breeze against your skin, and embrace the light that your eyes are frantically trying to adjust to? I suspect that for many of us, me included, the answer was anything.

If offered a way out of that dreamscape, I would not hesitate. So desperate to clutch onto any solution/escape, only to hear the door lock with blistering speed before I could even appreciate the word "free". Hours in the real world seemed like a great exchange compared to years in the other. What choice do you have when a system like that is designed to break you? When you are guilty as charged, guilty as non-charged, or even guilty of being suspected to be guilty, you just throw your hands up in defeat. So, once you have accepted your fate and understand the cold reality of mental incarceration, now what?

The good news is that there is a way out; the bad news is that the way is through. As with other sentences, the mental cage is intended to correct behavior and rehabilitate the individual, transforming them from an offender to a nonoffender. A sentence aims to prepare the person to be safely reintegrated into society — once again among others — trying to live safely, lawfully, and freely. At least, this is how it should work in an ideal situation.

Sometimes our minds are not as fair, just, or reformative as they can be. In the event that they are not, we are left to prove ourselves to ourselves. The justice that we seek within and the evidence that has to be presented to overturn the abjectly guilty label needs to be fueled by acceptance of what we are not, which are perfect beings. Embracing our humanity, accepting our flaws, and desiring to be better despite them is the key to the door that bars our way.

Am I the prisoner or the prison guard? We are the ones, at times, who hedge up the way and keep ourselves trapped, and at other times, the trapped, trying to set ourselves free. How can we be both the victim and the victimizer at the same time? How is it that we have such internal conflict within ourselves? How does one reconcile this, and why?

We incarcerate ourselves in our thoughts so that we can both process and resolve them. We also fight those same thoughts when we resist the changes necessary to correct past behaviors or feel unjustly maligned. Our past mistakes, our deepest regrets, and our true feelings lunge at us to where we at times may only feel safe in the cage. Identifying the reasons you are in the mental cage and being able to justify why you should not be is a difficult but necessary process.

When we can face those things we have been wanting to avoid, bury, and forget, we unlock ourselves and become free. The prison door exists at that point so people can come and go freely. Your access to the compound becomes limitless. The inside and the outside become one and the same, as you have access to everything. You can then work on anything and go anywhere. And, with proper transition, it becomes a place of solace, serenity, and freedom.

I had to take a very hard look at myself when I had no choice in the isolated state I was in. Thoughts that I had actively tried to compartmentalize and tuck away came right back to me. I had unfinished business with myself and needed to work with myself to get it done. To feel the emotions, go through the memories, and learn to be comfortable in my feelings felt good. To say the vulnerability I felt was tear-jerking is a vast understatement. Your mind can be a brutal and savage place, especially when you have been struggling to find control or accept the lack thereof. But through deliberate, purposeful, and intimate addressing of the issues at hand, I was able to hand myself the keys to my own cell, and you can too.

One can either be confined and pinned by their thoughts or liberated by them. Not addressing the thoughts through the various means at our disposal lengthens the time we remain in a prison and delays its transition into a sanctuary. Freedom can come through deep self-introspection, the aid of medication, and/or the reach of a confidante, family, or specialized professional. The journey itself varies in difficulty from person to person, but the bliss of a mind free to explore the

horizons of possibility within oneself is
worth it.

Chapter 4:

Incomplete

Experience:

To learn that I had been struck with a rare neuroimmunological disorder was one thing, but then to find out that I was not even the same kind of paraplegic I am used to seeing in the media was another. I thought that there would be no feeling, and I certainly thought there would be no pain. I thought I would be like the stereotypical character that could do something shocking to my legs, make people wince, and then laugh it off. I discovered really quickly, though, that I did not have that good fortune. To feel like my lower body has been soaked in cooking oil and then lit ablaze is a thought I tried to run from but failed for "obvious" reasons. I did not know that I could feel like my legs were a part of me, but also completely alien to my own body. When there is a disconnect between the brain and a part of the body, but a connection still exists between that part and the brain, it can actually run amok. There is nothing there to tell it to calm down, stop overreacting to everything, and stop interpreting everything as pain. It was really fascinating for being horrible, I thought. I have times when I feel like my legs may as well be sacks of sand, and other times when I feel like I could chill a bottle of water or be a really effective space heater. The lack of rhyme or reason had me questioning my own sanity a lot. I figured that I just finally lost the mental battle and was in a world of my own. A world closed off to the sense of the one we all live in. The laws of the world I perceived were unnatural and unfair. While getting used to the idea that I had perhaps lost my mind, I was disappointed to find out that I was somehow still lucid. What I thought I could perhaps escape through the rescue of therapy and medication was in fact reality. Hoping to lose my mind so that I would not be aware of the pains that never stopped was a wish I did not want to share with a single person. I thought that being lost or gone would be a mercy. I thought that not being able to feel would be a ticket to relief. I came to a point where I almost died again, this time due to a UTI that became a kidney infection. I found that my old pains started to feel overshadowed by my new pains. In a strange way, there was relief that I could experience something new. On the other hand, I knew that I was being overwhelmed by the full-body pain as a result of the septic shock. I found no peace in the idea that doctors were working feverishly to save my life. I found no relief in the idea that I would not suffer anymore, but rather regret that I had not done enough despite it. I survived with some damage and trauma that will follow me to my grave, whenever that will be, but I was changed. I realize that while I wish I could feel nothing, there are many paraplegics who wish they could feel anything. I discounted the progress that my body was attempting to make by trying to feel anything at all. I did not regard my condition as a hopeful step in the direction of recovery. I did not pay attention to my toes being able to move on and off, which, again, many wish they had. I did not regard having the ability to use the restroom as a triumph, whereas many are fighting to have continence restored to them. I allowed my pain, my fatigue, and my disappointment with my lack to overshadow and dismiss the good I had remaining. I now know that there are many different states of spinal cord injury, many levels, and even more subcategories. I am an incomplete paraplegic, and while it is a struggle only to feel pain in place of any sensation, I am grateful that I can feel something. I am grateful to have a life where I can feel anything, considering the alternative is literally nothing. I know people who have been overjoyed with less, and I know that I, too, can be happy since I already have more. The days of responding with, "but", this particular thing is barring me from being happy are over.

Reflection:

Some are so accustomed to the hunt that they can't appreciate the trophy. Some are so used to negativity that they can't accept positive things entering their lives. Some are so used to anger that they don't stop to feel happiness. The irony here is that we often act against our best interests when we're afraid to face changes in our lives. Doing something different, being treated differently, or seeing things differently can cause paralysis by analysis. Even when changes are beneficial, they can scare us so much that we don't move forward.

Being afraid of happiness because it ends the struggles that we are used to is difficult to grasp. Knowing how to deal with, suffer through, and complain about things in our lives is an actual comfort zone for people. Some of us have a poor sense of self-worth and cannot bring ourselves to accept good due to the guilt or shame we have about ourselves. Feeling undeserving or unworthy of the thing you seek most is a tragic example of self-defeat and self-sabotage.

Though I had sought to someday slow down and have more time to myself, the way that it came was not what I expected. Having my options become limited due to circumstances outside of my control made me feel cheated. Not being able to stop myself or slow myself down from achieving this goal felt wrong. I must have intended to tell myself that I would not get there, I would never work hard enough to deserve the rest, and that I only made it through out of sheer luck.

Why is it that we needlessly make our own lives harder by diminishing our own self-worth, minimizing our accomplishments, and discounting our hard work? There is humility, but there is also a deep-seated feeling that if we allow ourselves to be happy, something awful will happen. Maybe we feel that we can ruin anything, even happiness.

Maybe it is thought that it is better to deal with the disappointment we understand in bad circumstances than to open ourselves to possible new disappointments in good ones.

I realized that happiness and true satisfaction cannot be accepted outside until we reconcile what is going on inside. I realized that we could receive and receive good, but pass it off as nothing compared to what we think will be the big ticket. It seems we tend to look for big solutions to simple problems. Seeking happiness in the world at large to compensate for being unhappy with yourself is a losing battle we fight repeatedly for most of our lives.

How much money did we really have to spend on the house, the car, the clothes? How much time did we really need to spend on that project? How much energy did we need to spend preparing for that vacation? How much time do we need to spend away from our loved ones? How much money did we need to save? How much do we need to invest in our image for outward appearances? How much do we need to do to avoid having to face ourselves?

There is an entire school of thought that tells us that if we are surrounded by pleasing things, we will be able to fill the void within ourselves. The thought that if we have enough, do enough, see enough, buy enough, spend enough, and explore enough, we will be happy. While all these things can be nice and add pleasing elements to our lives, they are most certainly not enough to compensate for self-love.

If we loved ourselves enough, then we would realize much sooner that we already have enough, and that we already are enough. We would feel like we are good enough to deserve love and to be loved. We would realize we are strong enough because we would not dismiss the historical fact that we have faced challenges and still remain. We would realize that we are worthy of good things in our lives. We would realize that enough starts with inside, not out.

Lacking self-love will not just have us upset that it is raining, but also have us outside our home, wallowing in it instead of the shelter of self within. When you think about it, why would you expose yourself to unfavorable elements when you have a home wherein you can control your own environment? And if that is the case, then why care what is going on with the often-unpredictable weather patterns of life when you have consistent calm and comfort within? Do we live outside and just briefly brave the elements inside, or do we live inside and bravely venture out?

Chapter 5:

Quench

Experience:

I used to be extremely dependable and consistent. I used to be able to count on myself to do anything I wanted. My memory was nearly photographic; a flashbulb memory, they called it. I could remember things with incredible accuracy and had the pleasure of playing back memories whenever I wanted. How could all of this change seemingly overnight? A spinal cord injury isn't a concussive blow, but the fresh trauma somehow had a similar effect on my mind. I was haunted by the fear of just how much damage was done to me as I found myself losing myself. How could I start to forget even the faces of people I have spent so much time thinking about? I was used to forgetting to buy a gallon of milk or neglecting to pick up some other staple and laughing at myself for it, but forgetting people was ridiculous to me.

Naturally, I wanted to see just how much I had forgotten and how widespread it was, so I went to my library of TV shows and movies. I could read descriptions quickly and, like most people, determine whether I had seen them. Being excited about the summary would trigger my thoughts to go down memory lane and see if I had taken the journey through that story to its conclusion. I was an avid fan of many different titles and stories, as they offered a rich perspective that fueled my desire to understand people from all walks of life. I felt enlightened and connected by the images, stories, and lessons they held. Losing a story was akin to losing a lesson, which is akin to becoming vulnerable to making a mistake that could have been prevented by learning it otherwise.

I raided my watchlists, and to my mixed reaction, I found that I had many things in there that were super interesting and worth a watch, but I was only somewhat certain I had already seen some of them. I am sure there was a point in my life before where I wished that I could experience something for the very first time again, but this is not what I wanted it to be like. I wanted to feel the same thrill and amazement as when I watched a series for the first time or some of the best movies ever made. I know that life can be overwhelming and that we can grow to not be as excited about things we used to be when we were much younger, but again, this was different. At best, as I started watching some movies, I would remember that it seemed familiar at about 75% through the playthrough, and at worst, I watched things through 100%, and they were brand new to me.

I laughed at how amusing and scary my situation was. I used to laugh at the joke of the silver lining that someone with Alzheimer's could literally enjoy the same movie repeatedly, but this was not funny. While what I was experiencing was not nearly the same, it was similar enough to make me wonder again how much I had lost. I started to wonder how much I could learn over again, and just how long I could retain it before it would vanish as if it had never existed.

The situation was really strange and felt dismal to me as I kept grasping at memories that slipped through my fingers like smoke. One of the strangest things that happened to me when the neuroimmunological disorder called Transverse Myelitis struck me was another neurological condition that affected my sleep. Time already seemed to move very differently than it did before my injury, but the new normal that Non-24 Hour Sleep-Wake Disorder brought me to the brink of madness. My sleep schedule began to change every single day. Minutes to hours, each day was different, and I had no control over it. If I fought it, I would miss the sleep window that my body recognized and would be shut out from sleeping until the next window, which was usually about 24 hours from the last one. The windows I saw open each day seemed to shift by about an hour. So, if I started sleeping at 1 am today, then the next day I would feel the pull to sleep at 2 am, and the day after at 3 am, and so on. Over the course of a month, and every month, my sleep schedule would begin at every single one of the 24 hours in a day. Half the month I was awake during the day, and the other half during the night. This condition made it so that my internal clock was no longer synchronized with the rising and setting of the sun, as if I had become completely blind, yet I could still see.

Determined not to lose the rest of my precious memories, including, but not limited to, the faces of the people who mean the most to me, I purchased a digital photo frame. I was not willing to let my life be swallowed without a fight. I loaded image after image, memory after memory, and reminder after reminder. I started using note-taking apps on my phone and began writing down things I didn't want to forget. Having an idea of something I needed to do, forgetting it, and then remembering it 2 weeks later, if I was lucky, was not the way I wanted to live my life. I started acting on thoughts quickly so that I didn't give myself a chance to lose them.

I also determined that if I was going to lose the memories that made me happy, then I would just have to spend my life in fresh happiness and fresh experiences to make up for those that I could not recall. I wanted to get ahead of the loss rather than dwell on it. To my great surprise, it started to work. After years of falling into the same pattern of forget, neglect, and reflect, I took back control. The memories that I began to make started to stick. The sadness I felt for what was no longer found was eclipsed by the excitement of the happy moments I planned to experience. I realized that parts of me were gone and may never return for one reason or another, but it did not mean that I was alive to keep progressing.

Memories were gone, but I was not, not yet. Every single day is an opportunity to add more to the album of my life. Some may find joy in their past, and may live there, but I am choosing to live in my present and set up for the future. I cannot rest on my laurels anymore; I cannot depend on what used to be. My past is merely a reminder that I have every reason to create a legacy of wonderful experiences in my present and hopefully my future. Life is for living.

Reflection:

Have you ever noticed how draining life can be? There are a variety of ways to feel empty, and even extremes within each of those varieties. The cost of that depletion can be temporary at best and permanent at worst. There are times when we have the luxury of being prepared to recover and others when we are dealt an unfortunate blow.

I have not been particularly fortunate in avoiding some of the permanent consequences. Along with the paraplegia that stripped me of my ability to walk came compromised health that limited my social life and neurological issues that began to rob me of my memories. My perception of time was impacted in a strange way while I dealt with limited interactions, no time-bound goals, and the reality of fading relationships. It began to feel impossible to keep track of anything despite my very real desire to live as well as I could. Feeling despair for the lack of control I had, disappointment for what I could no longer accomplish, and sadness for the pieces of me that I knew were disappearing hit me hard.

I found myself struggling to remember some of the most important moments of my life. Day in and out, I have grasped at details I knew I should have remembered. I was really amazed at the casualties of self that were lost in this section of life's fog of war. It became easy to focus on the negative things and increasingly more difficult to stay fixed on the positive. The quiet moments were disturbed by booming thoughts of failure, regret, and sadness. My courage surrendered to fear, and my peace was lost in echoes of traumatic memories that threatened to deafen me from the inside out.

Isn't it tiring to search for peace in your current situation and constantly find war? Isn't it tiring having your progress, big or small, be arrested and put on trial by your self-perception? Where did the happiness that motivated me go? Where are the positive reinforcements I am calling on to win this conflict of will? How could I be losing the war within while still being armed with the experience of such a beautiful life?

I realized that I could not rest on my laurels and still be ok. I determined that my happiness was not simply to be found in my past, but also in my present and my future. I realized that I needed a balance and a constant flow to sustain me. Who I was is not who I am, and who I am is not who I will be. The thirst that was quenched yesterday does not satisfy the demands of today. The need to maintain and sustain became clear, and I knew what I needed to do. I realized that I was deserving of happiness and peace, but needed to fight for it. My life did not end when things grew more difficult, nor did my desire to be happy, or the ability to make it so.

I gathered tools to display the faces, places, and mental spaces I was inclined to forget. I needed reminders of who, what, and where to resurrect my best and happiest moments. Relying on tools and the inspiration from them then gave me confidence that all the future memories I was going to make would be secure as well. This is not to say that I ignored the quality of the time I planned to record just for the sake of recording it, either. I realized I could not live life unintentionally anymore; I needed to be acutely present in the moments. The quality of the time I captured was just as important as the act of recording it. What is the point of reliving something that is not real or creating a memory that I would not like to relive?

I can say with confidence that it is possible to live a very happy and full life, despite my struggles. Every time I see the faces of my loved ones, the laughter, the smiles, the environment, and the locations, I feel at home in myself. I feel like the cacophony of chaos is diminished to the point where I can only hear and physically feel the soothing embrace of a most welcome peace.

I have realized that it is crucial to make space in our lives for the happiness we seek. Devoting time to it, preparing for it, and protecting it is critical for our long-term satisfaction. If we are not committed to a cycle of living, remembering, and then repeating, then the happiness we thought would never fade loses its place in us. Being able to reflect on happy moments and take in their essence has helped me embrace life, face challenges, and more. It helped me realize that the patterns of my past can remind me how to live presently/intentionally, and the pattern of my present will help reinforce the cycle for my future.

Committing to live with full intention is key. Reconciling with the fact that life will not always be so happy helps in realizing the importance of genuinely enjoying the good times. Recognizing that I will not always be so strong has encouraged me to prepare for those moments of weakness by celebrating my moments of strength. Finding gratitude in sorrow, strength in discouragement, and present hope for future days is necessary to not lose ourselves in the delirium of negativity along the way.

Take photos, record the audio, notate the smell, dictate your experience, jot down some notes, and capture what you can. Whether your happy experiences are only spoons full, ladles, or a bucket, each drop counts when the rivers of abundance are affected by droughts of change. The inevitable thirst for the essence of happiness one has experienced is quenched by realization. Today is always a good day to remind yourself of the good, live for the better, and appreciate the now that will help you later.

Chapter 6:

Layered

Experience:

I was made to feel foolish for having the aspiration to make a difference. As I wondered how I could change my circumstances and do more, I was met with opposition that it was wishful thinking. My hopes and dreams were an afterthought and not taken seriously in the slightest. The idea that I could do more and contribute, helping others achieve their dreams and goals, was stalled by fear of judgment.

I regret that I listened to voices that said I could not instead of the voice inside that said that I can. I regret keeping company in my heart and mind that said I should remain in place instead of seeking those who knew I was ready to go. I regret embracing the comfort of complacency, cowardice, and ease rather than picking up the gauntlet and fighting the fight I was born to fight.

Denying who I was, so I could fit in, and not agitate those around me by my efforts to inspire change is a mistake I will never make again. I have made too many excuses for the things that I regret and denied the justifications for being the force for good that I knew I could be. What could have been was not, but that will not discourage or stop me from what will be.

I dreamed of being able to listen to people, talk to them, and help guide them on issues I had never even experienced myself. I believed that I did not need to have a mirror image of someone else's past to relate to them, much less show them compassion. I believed that being willing to understand would lead to the ability to understand, and I still do. I believed that devoting time to helping someone in need was a worthwhile investment, as doing good was its own reward. I believed that people could find the motivation to change if they identified it, and I still do.

I believe in the capacity to grow and leave our mistakes behind as we embrace a new life ahead of us. I believe this growth is a process per the timeline of the individual experiencing it, not dictated by societal standards. I believe that when someone is truly ready, then they will make the changes in their lives happen that they are prepared for. Our belief in others' ability to become more will couple with their own and encourage them when they begin the internal struggles necessary to emerge victorious.

It took me a long time to wake up, and now that I am, I will not rest until I have done as much good as I can with the talents, skills, and desire to make these dreams a reality. The scope of the impact is not my concern so much as the understanding that I have done something. And while my dream is maybe not the same as many others around me, I know that I will, for the right person, in the right place, bring the right things to their attention to inspire a change. It is then my deepest hope that they will turn around and do the same in their own unique way, creating a legacy of lifting up others who need someone to believe in them, too.

I am grateful for the friends I have made who have given to me and received the same in return, helping us all realize our potential. I do not want this beautiful and remarkable experience to end here, but to circulate and inspire many more. We cannot have come this far just to fall short of showing others why they should believe in themselves.

Reflection:

Have you ever had a dream so big and so life-defining that you would have sacrificed anything to achieve it? I had ambitions like that and laid out everything I knew to achieve my aims, except for a few parts of me. Have you ever accomplished something after working so long and so hard for it, only to be disappointed by not feeling, in the end, how you thought you would at the beginning? It is hard to build up to something so monumental in scope for your self-fulfillment, only to have it feel nice but empty.

I realized at some point that the thoughts of what I thought I wanted to be, discover, and accomplish were not actually my own. I realized that certain dreams and ambitions that I was in dogged pursuit of did not even matter to me. It hurts to realize that I had wasted time, energy, and considerable effort that I could have used to do what I actually wanted to do, or what I was meant to do. One of the chief regrets of mine has been my relationship with my family and how much pursuing these dreams cost me with them.

If what you are doing aligns very little with what makes you happy, then why torture yourself in doing it? This is the question many people would ask before being cut down by a reality that is framed largely by necessity, not idealism. However, is work really who we are, or is it just what we do? And if that is not self-defining, then what is? Moreover, who would know more about defining ourselves than ourselves?

Does fear hold us back from taking a deep dive into our minds to explore what we really want? Does fear of disappointment hold us back from trying? Does fear of change keep us from adapting to or evolving to meet our wants? Does doubt in ourselves keep us from building on the dreams that we have perhaps always had but never voiced out loud? What holds us back from having an honest sit-down with ourselves and planning to fulfill our utmost potential?

What do you want to be? What do you want to do? What do you want to change? How much time do you have to do it? When can you start?

Is there anything wrong with desiring to be a better parent? Is there anything wrong with desiring to be a better spouse, partner, or significant other? Is there anything wrong with desiring to help your local community better? Is there anything wrong with wanting to be a better person overall?

Beneath the exterior of the person who showed up to work and appeared to enjoy their job was my true passion, inspiring people. I was told that you could never make a living doing anything like that and that you should just stick to the tried-and-true industries. I have long since discovered that money from working was not the dream. I was not working for the money; I was working for the time so that I did not have to make more money. I was working to have time to spend with my family, my chosen family, and my community. I dreamed of inspiring others to get more out of their lives, more out of themselves, and to realize the happiness already around them.

Do we have to deny the part of ourselves that makes it all worthwhile in order to survive in this world? Is the price of survival truly the sale of our numerous gifts and talents? How are we to feel knowing that we are never going to fulfill the greatest part of ourselves?

I have found that while it is very taxing to find the strength, energy, and time to do those things that make us the happiest, we owe it to ourselves, our friends, and our family to try. We owe it to ourselves to make it a priority. We owe it to ourselves to gather ourselves in great measures and in small. We owe it to ourselves to protect ourselves from the elements that could dampen the effort. We owe it to ourselves to set our dreams alight and feel the surge of warmth by a blazing bonfire of joy.

When a controlled but brilliant fire is given life, it sends a signal to others near and far to come and see. We cannot help but notice, marvel, and start to desire to kindle the same within ourselves. We start to ask critical questions. If they could do it, then why can't I? What do I need to do to be as happy as they are? How do I fit this in my own life? Who will come to see me when I bring my dreams to life?

We are all made differently, none of us exactly the same, but we can recognize when someone has the fire of passion for what they love, radiating an undeniable, welcoming warmth. We have all caught sight of such a pillar, perhaps enjoyed the company of others around it, and wanted to see our own give life to other dreams alike. We all have the capability of seeking out our materials, combining them, preparing them, and finally igniting them.

What potential do you dream of fulfilling? What talents or gifts do you have to work with in order to get there? What do you need to develop those things? How do you begin? The question that should have the most obvious answer now is, why?

Chapter 7:

Growing Down

Experience:

You go there to live, and you go home to recover. They say this about hospitals, and in my experience, it has been true. Inconveniences like the food not being preferred, sleep being a rare luxury, and random people coming in at all hours of the day (some may or may not be constantly sticking you with needles), are a reminder that you would not be there if you did not have to be. There is also the matter of high costs and sometimes very unappealing experiences with those in charge of your care. I truly wish my experiences in a variety of emergency care settings were more positive, but instead, they have opened my eyes.

I have come across two kinds of people in all of my hospital experiences. One of those two is a compassionate, caring individual who treats you with dignity, respect, and integrity. The second is an individual who treats you as a nuisance between them and their break. It is shocking that I am more surprised by seeing the former than I am, by the latter. Although I can certainly understand that there are so many challenges that can test your motivations, you can outright forget or deny the reasons you chose to do what you do. While I can understand that people can become jaded and do awful things because of whatever they have going on inside, I cannot support them.

I did not enjoy having to contend with professionals who attempted to give me medication I did not authorize or was not informed about. I did not like being forgotten to be given a hospital bed for days. I did not like being slapped on the hand by someone who wanted to do something to my body their way, despite my discomfort. I did not enjoy being left in a location without help or transportation as a paraplegic without access to certain things like a bathroom or medication. I did not enjoy contacting a help desk, being ignored for several hours, and only having help come once alarms started going off, as my vital signs showed serious trouble.

It is interesting how you can be in a place designed to give you help, yet find that the intent and practice are at odds. It is also interesting how some people only did what they were supposed to do when there was a threat of enforcing policies or punishment of behaviors in front of them. And while I was suffering and struggling with whatever life-changing conditions I was facing at the time, I made it known that I was a human being just like the rest of them. Having to advocate for basic decency is something I never thought I would need to do in such a setting, but I have long since learned that many people do not regard others as they do themselves.

I wondered what had happened to them, or if they had always been that way. I asked myself what it would take for me to clock in for a paycheck and dismiss everything in between the clock-in and clock-out as irrelevant details. I wondered if, in their shoes, I could have justified treating myself and others with such disregard.

I do not know what it is like to work as a doctor, nurse, lab tech, neurologist, anesthesiologist, or any of the numerous titles I encountered during my stays. I do, however, know that the title that demands respect and courtesy from all of us equally is that of being a human being. I could have equally treated those in charge of my care as unwell as they treated me, or gone on to assume every new experience would be the same, but I did not. The minority that showed their true colors to be impassioned to do the right thing, determined to save lives, and motivated to turn a negative time into a positive one, inspired me.

I suspect that the hope of the compassionate is that they will be met with compassion during their moments of weakness. I also suspect that the compassionate know that it is not if they will someday need help, so much as when they will need it. I am also inclined to believe that the opposite forgets or denies the reality that they could and, in all likelihood, will someday need help themselves. I was reminded to treat others as I want to be treated because we are all one and the same. And while my condition and my situation are certainly rare, my desire to live the best I can in my humanity is most certainly not.

Reflection:

I have always heard that growing older is one of the hardest things we can experience in our lives, but I would say that growing wiser feels harder still. It is definitely true that one can grow old without ever growing up. We can easily pass the time without accounting for it regardless of whether we do or do not try hard enough.

Imagine being a tree that has been growing for 35 years, only to be blown down by a mild storm? You are vibrant, tall, and look relatively healthy compared to all the other trees, and yet you are gone at the mildest threat. What is the difference between the trees that remain upright and those that fail to live out more fulfilling lives? The root system.

How deep do the roots go? How far apart do they spread? How diverse are the underground paths in which they are expanding and communicating? How hard is the tree working to ensure that all the progress at the top is not lost due to light work at the bottom? How well is the tree communicating, not just with itself but with others along the way?

We can grow and grow for show while displaying all manner of fruits, ecosystems we sustain, and the beautiful potential in us, only to be knocked down after some clouds gather. So, how does one stay intact? There needs to be a healthy balance between the roots and the branches. An appreciation for what is done on one end and an appreciation for what is done on the other. All parts work in tandem to create a sturdy and enduring entity.

Why do the roots envy the branches, and the branches mock the roots? What is to be said of humility, civility, equality, and compassion for the whole and not just the part? What qualifies one to be better than the other? Do we not all take from the same source, require the same sustenance, and are subject to all the same changes and transitions? Do we differ so much that we truly feel entitled to different treatment? Does seeing the sunrise one hour sooner make all the difference, or seeing the sunset later? Can one drink water better than another to the point where we can declare them superior?

We can become so fixated on trying to separate ourselves from others and elevate ourselves above them that we lose sight of our humanity. When we forget the purpose of the whole, or in other words, the unity aimed at improving our lives, we begin to drain ourselves of a vital element: happiness. If we justify all the reasons we shouldn't have to change, listen, stay open-minded, or grow, then we stagnate and begin to die. But why die when we can live?

Is a branch at the top still superior, as it and the rest of the tree it is attached to come down? How will that branch be remembered in conjunction with the rest of the tree? Will there be special honors for all the superior branches? Will there be honorable mentions for the superior of each tree that is downed by age or by a random act of nature? Acting superior is vital to the establishment and survival of the tree, is it not? Reputation and image, not productivity, is the way, correct?

Inequality, condescension, and browbeating are how things get done. There is no such thing as a better way, not while all of these long-established behaviors have produced true winners. Without a designated winner and clearly labeled losers, we would not know who is superior and who is not.

And what is to be said of the older, frail, or infirm? What value do they have, and where do they fall in this hierarchy? What happens if we are privileged to live long enough to become a part of that group? Is it a privilege to live a relatively short life instead? What is superior or inferior? And who deems it so?

While we mull these very pressing and important questions, there are many other issues pressing upon humanity. We are experiencing loneliness, loss, sadness, hunger, disease, and distress of every kind. While we have so many important questions about perceived outward status, many of us are fighting battles that the eye cannot see. And while we tend to focus on the things that we cannot change, there are countless ways that we can support one another. Should we appeal to our humanity when we can simply focus all of our attention on our vanity?

Maybe the idea of respect, courtesy, compassion, and humility is only fit for those who live long enough to appreciate it? Perhaps the idea of equality cannot possibly exist amongst all the various states and stages of life we're in. After all, what we have in common should be the determining factor for what matters most, right? And if that is the case, then what do we have in common? Do we have concerns, needs, dreams, goals, and a time/energy limit for addressing them? Lastly, are we ever interrupted by unexpected matters so pressing that they put those concerns, needs, dreams, and goals on low priority?

How many of us grow up but never grow down? How many of us grow for length but not for depth? Do you grow

for show and neglect your roots? Some of

us grow wise, and some grow otherwise.

Chapter 8:

Running to Running From

Experience:

The lies I told myself to do the right thing for the wrong reason punished me. Those lies compounded until I convinced myself that I could never have enough, I could never put in enough hours, and nothing I could do would ever be enough. My beloved workaholic tendencies were not born of necessity but of pride and insecurity.

I never minded working extra shifts because they meant extra money. I grew up in hard times where you could not always guarantee that needs would be met even if you sacrificed for it. I grew accustomed to my parents toiling and clawing for every inch they could gain. The savagery of survival and the constant drive to get ahead and stay ahead were imprinted on me from a young age. I could never speak ill of how hard my family had to work to establish themselves and blaze a trail for me as a 1st-generation American. I do not envy anyone who has had to start from nothing and create everything out of grit, nonstop hard work, and sacrifices, including obligations to those closest to them. I did not imagine that my path would even come close to as arduous as my parents', or as solitary.

As I grieved for not being able to work like I used to, think as I used to, and show up like I used to, I realized something awful. I did not have to do all that I did to make a living, and I did not do everything that I could have to make a home. I could have worked fewer hours and had sufficient for my needs. I could have taken time away from work instead of priding myself on never taking a vacation, for fear of losing money. The ones and zeros offered me no comfort when my life was turned upside down, and the memories of work were just as cold. Instead, all I could think of was what I would have done if I could have gone back. I am haunted by the smiles I could have shared, the laughter I could have enjoyed, the experiences I could have embraced, and the memories I could have made. While I am grateful that my loved ones did not abandon me despite my own selfishness, I have felt deeply ashamed that it took all of this for me to realize their worth to me. I sold the time that they could have had me present to glut my pride and ego. I broke promises that I would only do enough to make sure we were secure financially, and in turn, robbed my loved ones emotionally.

I played the part of the hero, rushing off to rescue the day for my clients first and then my family second, without realizing that I was becoming a villain. Justifying my neglect of the balance between too little, too much, and enough cost me dearly. Relationships that perhaps could have survived with the right amount of attention and intention were lost. Awareness of problems I could have addressed before they became significant, and damaging would have been there if I had made the time. Heartache that could have been quelled sooner instead drew on further, culminating in acute pain and regret. I am grateful that I now have only a fraction of the regret that I would have had if I had been able to continue. I have cause to pause, reflect, and course correct. Those I have in my life are worth more to me than I feel I deserve, and I owe it to them to give them something more valuable than my pride, my ego, and money; my time.

Reflection:

As I reclined in my broken chair, staring at the ceiling, I wondered what my life would have been like if I weren't as broken as my seat. I questioned what my future might have been if I hadn't been knocked off course. As I drift into unknown parts, it occurred to me that, although mysterious in nature, the path ahead may not be worse than what could have been. I say this while giving myself credit for working hard while I was able-bodied, doing kind deeds for others when I had the chance, and making sacrifices for family and friends alike. I aimed to be generous, kind, and supportive at home in whatever way I could. I took that responsibility as seriously as most would by providing for their home and ensuring security.

While I was at work, I worked as hard as I could. So hard in fact that it was difficult to leave things left undone for the next workday. I felt guilty for not getting things done as early and as far ahead as possible. My mark as a professional was always to be timely, efficient, and worthy of recommendation.

I knew that in my field of expertise, job security, and advancement depended on how much of myself I threw into the job. It was not unrealistic to feel like I had very little left to give when I arrived home after a long day. It was not so uncommon once upon a time for me to work 70 to 90+ hours a week. After all, to be the best, you had to be there the most, or so I thought anyway. There was nothing I could be doing better for my family than working hard every single day and pouring every ounce of focus, energy, and wit into my career. If you want to go far, you need to go further than your coworkers. If you want to be the boss, then you need to come in early and stay late. Winners always win, with no exceptions.

I bought into the work part of work ethic, but did not really go much further into understanding why I needed to work as I did. Why did I need to work in excess of 90 hours a week and still bring my work home with me on occasion? Why did I need to stay late as often as I did when I knew that no matter how hard I worked, there would always be a stack of tasks waiting for me? Why did I decide to go in early when I knew I could reasonably accomplish the task within regular business hours? Was I afraid of not accomplishing enough at work, or was I afraid of acknowledging what I was not accomplishing at home?

There is a very big difference between what we need and what we want. How much do I need to set aside to cover my obligations? How much do I want to satisfy my pride? How much do I need to feel accomplished? How much do I want to be recognized as "most accomplished"? How much time do I need to spend at work? How much time do I want to spend away from home? How much of myself do I need to dedicate? How much of myself do I want to? After all, there are only so many hours in a day, and why would we waste our time pouring into things that don't bring us value? It occurred to me that although I said I was working like I was for the sake of my family, I was in fact working for myself.

I only realized this when I started taking an inventory of what I was thinking about before, during, and after my chosen obsession, or in this case, work. I also started analyzing my level of enthusiasm for beginning or ending every other task that was not my chosen obsession. Realizing that I did not move as quickly to attend to other things struck a chord with me. To also realize that I moved particularly slowly about leaving the thing I wanted most made me start to question my priorities. Who has time to question their priorities? Why would anyone want to stop and re-evaluate when it is so much easier to just keep doing what we know best?

Life is like a weapon, and we are the marksmen. We only have so much ammunition to deploy into our chosen targets. The ammunition we carry is time, and we never seem to have enough. It cannot be created, cannot be reused, and is so limited, in fact, that we do not know at any point when we will receive any more. These factors make the use of the ammunition more important with each shot that we take. Knowing that our shots will run out encourages us to fire. Remembering that our shots will run out, sharpens our aim. What are we hitting? What are we missing?

I, for one, found out the hard way that family is very real and relevant in times of crisis. And during those times when crisis unites them in one focused effort (how it often does happen), we get a glimpse of the strength of the relationships we have with each member. During the tough times, we refocus on the generosity, kindness, and selflessness of those who come to our aid. We may even envision a scenario where we can have familial relationships on this level all the time, without an emergency.

So, why don't we focus on those permanent titles of sibling, parent, child, bonus parent, or otherwise, vs the other titles where we are easily replaceable? Why don't we spend more time on what we are rather than what we do? What do we have to show for failing in lifelong relationships, successfully completing an accomplished career, and then facing the obscurity of retired life, alone? I suspect that those who arrive at that point, battered, broken, tired, or any of the adjectives fitting someone who is no longer able to perform their job, feel regret. After all, what does anyone have to look forward to after their work life comes to an end? Who do they have to look forward to? Who will be there to comfort them when they lack purpose, are in pain, lack self-esteem, and feel they have no more value?

What are you running to every day? What are you running from? Could it be that we have it backwards, and we should invest more into our relationships than into our fascinations? I find great comfort in knowing that I can correct my regret by building stronger relationships with my loved ones, now. I take solace in knowing I didn't discover, after a long career and much effort, that the most important thing to me was not the work, but the people I was working for. This means my family, whether biological or chosen, is the reason I did what I did. I could have dedicated less or more time to various areas. Ultimately, I'm glad it's all come full circle, and I realized I should have been working for the time to spend with family, my actual treasure. What are you spending your time on, and does it truly make you happy? If not, stop, reevaluate, choose, and then move like time does not come back.

Chapter 9:

Why Do We Fear

Experience:

This book has been a project that forced me to face many fears. Among those was the fear that I was asking questions people did not need/want answers to, talking about things they were not interested in knowing, and experiencing things they saw no value in understanding.

For 8 years, I reflected on all the principles and thoughts I could reasonably share. For 8 years, I tested my ideas and judged whether they were a waste or wisdom. For 8 years, I dreamed of hearing just one person say, "Thank you, you've saved me a lot of time and pain." For 8 years, I learned from my past, reconciled with my present, and prepared as best as I could for a better future. For 8 years, I worked to convert pain to power, pity to persistence, and pandemonium to peace. For 8 years, I imagined what it would feel like to finally hold all the important lessons I learned. For 8 years, I tried to see how this short book could help someone else live a fuller, more well-rounded life.

There is a time for thinking, and there is a time for action. I recognized that the time for me to act on what I had learned had come. I recognized that I did not want to let another moment go by where that dream of helping someone else through my words could not come true. I realized that we cannot live in fear and are truly made alive in courage. The balance for a life well lived rests on the point of the double-edged sword, Caution and Action. Too much caution and no action leads to unrealized potential, while too much action and no caution leads to regret for failing to respect possibilities. A motivation to take a swing, follow through, and live fully is key. My fear for what may be said, how I may be judged, and how I may fail no longer holds me back. My body, though traumatized and damaged, will follow my mind, and my mind is now made free.

Reflection:

Have you ever been so afraid of making a mistake that you are paralyzed by it? That is to say that the thought of change for the worse keeps you from doing anything, even with the chance of things getting better. You realize that it is irrational, but you still find yourself feeling helpless, hopeless, and lost.

I have been on a path that has had many twists and turns, some of my own making, and others an ever-repeating lesson in life's ability to surprise you. I have made mistakes that I wish I did not have to carry the striking lessons from. A number of these lessons even came from painful repetitions of the same course. Life can be a very merciless teacher, and with good reason. I would love to think that I was intelligent and learned fast, but in hindsight, I was a glutton for punishment and learned very slowly.

I suspect that many of us fall into the same category: repeat students. We spend a lifetime relearning very painful and often expensive lessons. The cost of this education can be financially challenging, emotionally devastating, and physically debilitating, just to name a few extremes. And so why isn't it wise to just pause and do nothing at all when repeating the same tests we've had in the past? Isn't not answering the questions better than answering and getting them wrong?

Is this why it is easy to stray from commitments? If one does not commit, then there are no consequences to inaction? If one does not respond, then there is no consequence to silence, for who can take fault in no answer? If one simply does not act when acted upon, then is there nothing to say, and the situation, whatever it may be, is resolved?

I know all too well that these are coping mechanisms that ultimately reinforce the very guilt you are trying to avoid, given the very real consequences of checking out of our lives. Removing ourselves, even just consciously, does not stop the decision-making process, and it does not stop the real clock in the real world from ticking. While it sounds cliché, it is very true that if we do not make our decisions in time, time makes the decisions for us. Thus, relief in avoiding choice, is always replaced by discomfort in the unavoidable consequences.

How can we be expected to make a choice when it seems like all the choices at our disposal are laden with undesirable consequences? I would say the first thing to do is set aside our pride. It may not make sense at first, but the very first lesson here is to learn from others who have passed the test before you.

Can we be so determined to face life's lessons by ourselves that we sabotage ourselves? I think the answer is a resounding yes. What do we tend to be afraid of in relying on others for help this way? Do we think they may misdirect us because they have a vested interest in our failure? Are we afraid of what they may think of us, that they will think less of us for not knowing what we do not know? Are we afraid that we will be judged for having weaknesses that we attempt to hide? Are we afraid to show everyone else that we are all, in fact, human, each of us in need of help? When did acting like we know what we are doing become the rule and not the exception?

Is societal pressure to be, look, or act a certain way more commonplace than we realize? Does it seem to have compounded over time? Does it feel like it is essential to lie about our qualifications for the jobs we want? Is dishonesty about what we do know more acceptable in society than honesty about what we do not? Are we emotionally cruising by on life's tests while not actually obtaining its crucial education?

It is a peculiar irony when a display of strength is weakness, and a display of weakness is strength. We should be lifelong students, educating ourselves in various areas. To put off learning/applying the lessons life must teach us is to invite foolishness to chase away wisdom. If our lack of knowledge distracts us from the pursuit, we are doomed to stagnation. We cannot become smarter, stronger, wiser, and truly happy if we do not endeavor to learn. A bucket in a shed may help you address your thirst, but it will never quench it. Imagining going out to get the water will not make it materialize. Finally, deciding not to drink the water retrieved will leave you thirsty still.

Even indecision is a decision, no matter how much we wish it were not so.

Putting off a choice, no matter the reason, is a choice. When we do not answer, we have in fact responded with silence. The question to ask at this point is, are you willing to accept the regret of indecision or risk being happy with a choice?

Every decision, good or bad, has led you to where you are right now. Every triumph and every defeat has shaped a curve, a turn, an incline, and a decline. Every choice has added to the length of your path.

There have likely been times when certain regrets have made us feel like there would be no more road ahead. In shame, perhaps we thought we would die and could not bear the idea of life going forward. In embarrassment, we may have wished that we were buried lest anyone realize the scope of the consequences of our decision. In fear, we may have thought that there is no more certainty or security, and therefore everything was coming to an end.

The reality is that life did not end during our first regret, second, third, or even fourth. I would wager that many of us make mistakes at least once a month, if not once a day. Those mistakes did not stop time, and they should not stop you from making more decisions in time. Choosing your path leads to a fulfilling life, no matter the consequences, whereas avoiding choices leads to a hollow existence, void of intentional happiness.

Why avoid the risk of being happy for the certainty of regret? You are already living with regret, have likely learned a thing or two, and can now do better. Why learn, if not to succeed where you have failed? Why not try for positive through a choice of your own making, rather than settle for the negative? Why do we keep walking the path, despite all the mistakes and regrettable moments, if not in search of some happiness ahead? If we are going to fail, like we most certainly have, then we fail forward, 10, 20, 30, 40, 50+ times, ad infinitum, until we succeed. What we learn from engaging with, and disengaging from, our choices, successes, and failures alike is how to live and why we live.

Chapter 10:

The Value Theory

Experience:

People have overlooked me or said, "Don't worry, maybe you can still do the things you used to do." Was I better than I am now?

I have been told that many people feel sorry for me because I can't do the job I used to do. I have been asked why I am not able to do the same work or focus to the same degree. I have been questioned about the extent to which my disability has prevented me from participating in my old life. When I laid out all the answers, I was looked upon with pity, as if there was nothing left for me in this world. It was as if I had nothing left to live for if I could not resume life as it had been. It felt as if I were being talked about in the past tense, as if there were nothing left for me in the present or the future.

I was made to feel that it was all downhill from here. However, instead of regretting what was, I started to embrace what is. The way ahead was difficult because it was so hard to digest the idea that I had nothing by society's standards to show for my time. Letting go of the idea that my value and, therefore, my potential rests in material things is the best thing that could have happened.

I placed value in my peace, persistence, and patience, which began with realizing that I am still the same person who accomplished all I ever did. I am the same person who managed to come this far and through all the difficulties life has thrown my way. I am still here. I have not been erased, and my story is not over. Every single day is an opportunity to add more, try a little harder, and recognize the things I should be grateful for.

I have stretched and grown far beyond what I thought I was capable of. I continue to adapt and accept the new limitations in place of the old ones. I screamed in victory and cried, "I will never give up", once. I have not forgotten where I was as I sobbed into the water raining down from above me. The water was cold, but my chest was alight like a hot furnace, the skin on the back of my neck and arms raised, the heat radiated down back and sprinted across my body. The clarity I received, that I was, and therefore am limitless, despite my limits, changed me. And the only question that I had after I realized who I am was, what am I going to do about it?

Reflection:

Have you ever been judged based on what you do, don't do, want to do, don't want to do, and so on? I have found some very compassionate people who have treated me as a person, even in hard times, and others who have treated me like the dirt beneath their shoes. I wondered why some people could see me as a human being, and others could not even begin to associate me with humanity. I have even had others not recognize me outside of work, just as suddenly as we were no longer in the same daily environment. How is it that we can disassociate so much that we are not even able to recognize each other? Is it terrible that I started to believe that if I was not in the right place, the right position, or achieving the right thing, I was as worthless as the onlookers thought I was? Being confined to a wheelchair, laden with memory issues, struggling with neurological misfires, and a host of pains that come through spinal cord injuries made me feel like a nobody.

I found myself unrecognizable without my possessions, my titles, and the resources from my work to support those things. I felt like I was an imposter, a fake version of the successful, happy, and functional person that I once was. I felt like all the things that had made me someone were taken away, and all that remained was the husk, barely resembling who I was. What was I without all the knowledge I had to back my certifications? What was I without all my licenses? What was I without all the boundless energy to see my chosen projects to completion? What was I without the ability to make the money my family needed to make ends meet? What was I, if not a provider, a breadwinner, a champion of the workplace, a respected member of my associates, and overall perceived winner in the rat race? How could I live with myself if I did not even respect myself? How could I care about or want to regard my own needs when I did not feel like I deserved anything? How could I be expected to think about the future, much less the present, when I was still grieving who I was until the recent past?

Increasingly, I felt isolated as all of those who once called me constantly seemed to have moved on and forgotten about me. They too figured that the me that was clad in success, a professional image, and the unstoppable confidence that came with it had died. They, however, did not mourn or send flowers; instead, they replaced me in their minds with another who filled my place. How was it that despite how good I was at what I did, how good I was to them, and how unique I was, they did not even remember me after a short while? How was it that all these people that I called my friends did not even pay me the same courtesy you would give to a stranger? The kicker, though, is that I was in fact still alive, just barely, and now I had no purpose and no name.

When I say I had no purpose and no name, I mean I was adrift and really lost about my place in this world. My background, my successes, my career, and my laser focus on those things were my anchor. Without them, I had gotten tossed by wave after wave of disappointment and set on a course to meet some uncertain end far from the safety of the harbor I used to know. I lost the will even to try to move in any direction, as my will felt powerless against the strength of the currents that were pulling me. Does the ship define the captain, or does the captain define the ship? Does a crew set sail because of the ship, or do they set sail because of who commands the ship?

Surprisingly, despite the many who forgot my name, I was still remembered by a select few. How was it that they remembered me when even I did not remember myself? When I say myself, I mean the person that preceded all I had achieved. They looked upon me and did not identify me by my colors, my shiny trinkets, the vibrant sails, the fancy writing, and all the things that I thought defined me as worthy. To my great astonishment, they did not care about any of those things and just saw me as one of them without exception.

My true family and friends saw someone in me that I did not even recognize anymore, much less respect. The person they saw may have been well-intentioned, kind, considerate, and loving, but those qualities did not pay the bills. The person they saw in me would certainly give the shirt off their back to them, but that same person would not be able to afford to buy another one. The person they knew was nice, but worthless in many ways, according to what I had come to know. The person underneath was not deserving of loyalty, at least not like I used to have.

It turns out that I was wrong again on this. My family would invite me to dinner and not even ask about the businessman. My friends would invite me to activities and did not even inquire about what was going on in my office. My family did not even bother to ask about my online presence or how my quarterly reports were looking. Looking back, I am flabbergasted that they did not ask and did not care. How could these people who purport to love and care about me be so indifferent about what I did for a living? If that was not important to them or valuable, then what was?

In the ensuing conversations I had with them about the past, present, and future, they told me how much they loved me, how proud they were of me, and how special I was. They had stayed with me and even embraced me more now, even though I had not made nearly the same amount of time to speak to them back then. They were encouraging me, nurturing me, feeding me, and tending to my every need, even without asking. How is it that these guys could see me number one, and number two, how could I see myself in the same way?

They reminisced about my much younger days and talked about how they have always loved my laughter, my smile, and my desire to bring both laughter and smiles to others. They talked about how they always appreciated my willingness to lend a hand, no matter the task. They talked about me being a kind soul for always befriending those I saw who had no friends. They spoke to me as if no time had passed by. As if they could see the younger version of me that believed in all those things.

They saw that I was not smiling and reminded me that I was smiling before I ever had teeth. They reminded me that they loved me before I ever accomplished anything in this world and would continue to do so, irrespective of whether I ever did again. They reminded me that I laughed all the time, had fun, was vibrant, and excited. Was that version of me truly dead, like the professional alter ego I had assumed over the years? In conflict, I asked myself, which part of me has my sudden illness and its devastating effect brought to an end? I knew that the me I wanted to portray was gone, and the me that remained was a version I did not recognize, like, or respect. Why would anyone want to embrace this version of me, what with all the weakness, lack of power, and lack of ability to work?

The response came in waves as I reflected on who I was before becoming who I am. I knew how to smile before I made my first dollar. My friends and family made me smile without ever presenting me with money, an opportunity, or a promotion. I knew how to smile before I ever donned any graduation caps, framed any certificates, or received any bonuses. I most certainly knew how to smile before I ever heard of the word quota, obligation, rent, or mortgage, to name a few. And now what? Will I never smile again, or will I rediscover the reasons that I have always had? And if I can rediscover these reasons, then how?

The people who truly know us will remind us of who we are at every turn. Their interactions with us, their gestures, their body language, and even their desires regarding physical, mental, and emotional proximity. Their finding value in us, where our regular interactants would not, is another sign. Perhaps most significant is the steady intensity of their love for us that is clearly seen in their eyes. Looking further still, we glimpse what they see when they look at us. And if it was lost upon us that we are lovable, can also love ourselves, can nurture ourselves, and choose happiness because of it, then no more.

Is it a revelation that we discover when our loved ones come around and tell us about ourselves, or is it a reminder? Should we put more stock in those who would abandon us the moment we are no longer conveniently a part of their story, or should we believe those who have always chosen to be a part of ours? And is our true value based on those who flee or those who remain during the difficult moments? Are we expendable, replaceable, and common? Is our time, energy, heart, and effort for sale? What is our value, and who determines it? What is the value of a life?

I know that my worth is beyond money, objects, or time in the eyes of those who love me, who, in turn, taught me to love myself. I know that my presence to them is incalculable. I know that the essence of who one is transcends understanding in those who can have the heart to see it truly. And because I can see the value in me, I can now also fully realize the value in others. Therefore, I have chosen to be an pillar for my friends, my family, and those who can appreciate who and what I am. I would rather have little value to the world at large and infinite value to my dear ones at small. I know that if anyone takes the time to get to know beyond the external appearance, they can discover what makes the heart's drum beat, the mind's clock tick, and all the interactions that need no words, powerful. What is your worth? And if you assign a number to that value, then, are you bought or are you sold?

Chapter 11:

Understanding Intent

Experience:

I was betrayed despite the time and energy I devoted. It made me stronger.

I found myself so lost, so cold, and so sad that I just wanted vanish. The pain was so exhausting that I felt like I had nothing left to give despite life asking for more. My nerves were so past reeling that I could not even process the shock. I experienced such loss that I started to question the meaning of my existence. I poured my entire self in, only to feel the ground's rugged embrace when the cup was tipped over.

The intensity of betrayal by someone so close to my heart wracked my body with pain. I could not breathe without stifling tears. I choked on memories that came streaming back with no mercy. I searched and searched for where I went wrong and how I arrived here. I thought I knew better, I thought I was safe, and I thought a foundation of trust so strong could never crack.

What was sadness grew into frustration and then anger at the thought of what was taken from me. My time, my thoughts, my energy, all lost. The trust I invested, the promises, all to waste. And now I have to start over, assuming I recover. These were my thoughts and more as I struggled to reconcile my feelings of grief. And though I felt that parts of me could not ever come to be put back together, they did. My desire to live was stronger than my desire to surrender to loss. My desire to continue was stronger than my desire to stop. And the realization came that the best was still yet to come.

The parts of me that I thought were taken were still, in fact, here. As it turns out, they could not be stolen, only borrowed. The experiences that had shaped me and made me were my own. The heart that pumps the life-rich blood through my veins still belonged to me. The center of operations in my head had not ceased. I was the same, but different. I had a weakness, but also a new strength. I experienced failure, but a surging determination to overcome it took over.

Reflection:

Rebuilding yourself is not easy, as it requires time, effort, and community. I was very alone in my thoughts at some points, but gradually came out changed, excited, yearning, hopeful, and vulnerable at the same time. For me, the weight of my past began to lift, and my confidence began to return. It felt as if I had been hiding away from the world for quite some time and then emerged from my solitude, ready to engage once more. Have you ever been so excited that you could not wait to interact and begin something new? Have you ever come away from loneliness, grief, sadness, or despair, just wanting to embrace a loving, comforting, and encouraging world? Have you ever been given reasons why this is not a good idea?

It is not unreasonable to have a healthy fear of what others may do, as their intentions are not exactly painted on their faces. I know that I am not built like a human lie detector, and I wish that I had been at certain points in my life. I wish that I could have advocated for myself then as I could do so now. I wish I could have detected the signs or picked up on indicators that I had invested in a loss. Learning painful lessons because of trusting the wrong people is not for the faint of heart. Many of us do not come away from difficult betrayals fully intact with our faith in humanity. Should we remain secluded, never rely on people, board up the door of trust, and, for good measure, throw away the key?

Despite how much I disliked the idea of letting others in, I realized that it was a luxury that no one could afford. Everyone, everywhere, needs someone for something. We are simply not meant to be on our own, nor should we have to be.

There have been times in my life when I brushed off the need for interaction to avoid risking my trust. Who wants to repeat the cycle of disappointment after experiencing the pain of losing a friend, losing a lover, or any other close relationship? Beyond the personal, the world is full of those who would commit fraud, scam, or lie to steal your assets without hesitation. No matter what we may feel like we lack, someone, somewhere, will always want what we have. Whether you are well and put together or struggling and just trying to survive, you hold value, and someone is intent on using you for a purpose.

So, the very thought of having to trust someone who may not have been safe was too much. However, as I delayed dealing with the discomfort, I put myself in a worse position by having to make a reflexive decision, quickly. I then leaped out of desperation because the priority of my needs had exceeded my desire to avoid the risk.

You may be able to guess where this has led me, but to be clear, it ends up in failure. In fact, it further eroded my self-confidence in making good decisions and reinforced my lack of faith in people. This then made me more apprehensive about trusting others again. I put myself in an emotional spin cycle with a broken timer.

What is the solution to the me-or-them problem? You can only really control your part in the interactions and filter who you allow into your life. The key I found was that if I make myself available, then they will come to me, not me rushing to them. And if I, being an honest person, desire honest people in my life, then I need not be afraid to verify them. Are you not worth confirming that your heart, energy, effort, and time are being used with the right people? Is it better to take the risk of avoiding trust until the last second or judge for yourself after learning how? I believe it is good to trust, but it is better to verify that your trust is not misplaced. Sometimes we are pride, and sometimes we are prey.

Knowing where we stand in this wild world is one of the best ways not only to survive but thrive.

The test is relatively simple. When we are being pursued, we need to be bold enough to ask them why until we have a good idea of who they are and what they are. They have tracked you down and identified you for reasons yet unknown, so it is only fitting that they identify themselves. They want to present an opportunity. Ask why? They want to date you. Ask why? They want to give you something. Ask why? If you have questions about what they are doing or who they are, then you are entitled to ask them to help you understand. If a party expects you to be vulnerable to them, then they need to be vulnerable to you. They may not expect you to want to know or ask about what they are doing, why they are the way they are, and/or why they chose to pursue you. However strange it may be, if they are engaging you, then you need to engage them. The trust you want to give, or reserve, should be earned, not surrendered. You should feel satisfied enough with the exchange that you feel good about your decision to let them in or keep them out. You have very good reasons for wanting to protect your interests, and so they need to have very good reasons as to why you do not have to.

No matter your setbacks, advancements, losses, victories, abilities, inabilities, talents, or lack thereof, you are someone in this world. Everyone needs someone! We will come across trustworthy and seedy alike. We cannot stop living our lives or denying the best parts of ourselves. To give is to live and to live is to give. Navigating the risk of misplaced trust is not only necessary, but worthwhile to find the joy that comes through those that are worthy of it. We have come too far and have either seen or have yet to see too much to be spectators in our own lives. We need to be active in pursuing a better life, supporting our people, our village, our community, and investing in a happy future for them.

We cannot afford to hide behind the daily hustle and bustle. We cannot afford to make excuses for not attempting anymore. We can have a healthy respect for the more dangerous aspects of the world. However, we cannot let fear of those aspects flood our minds, washing away our potential, goals, and resolve to move forward. Every single day is a gift, as evidenced by the many we see and know who no longer receive it. We need to treat it as such, take hold of what we have, who we have, for as long as we have, and live today, every single day. Be new, be bold, be alive! If that is a struggle and you need more reminders, then go back and read through again, spend time with your loved ones, and ask yourself what life would be like without them. You will find the answers you are looking for. And finally, you will find the resolve to make the changes you will realize need to be made.

Afterword

Finding clarity in confusion and order in the chaos of life is no easy task, but is worthwhile. May you continue to find strength in weakness, inspiration in awareness, purpose in peace, and joy in your journey.